S. HRG. 113–468

BRINGING OUR TRANSIT INFRASTRUCTURE TO A STATE OF GOOD REPAIR

HEARING

BEFORE THE

SUBCOMMITTEE ON HOUSING, TRANSPORTATION, AND COMMUNITY DEVELOPMENT

OF THE

COMMITTEE ON BANKING, HOUSING, AND URBAN AFFAIRS UNITED STATES SENATE

ONE HUNDRED THIRTEENTH CONGRESS

SECOND SESSION

ON

EXAMINING THE STATE-OF-GOOD-REPAIR NEEDS OF THE NATION'S TRANSIT INFRASTRUCTURE, AND THE FEDERAL ROLE IN ADDRESSING THESE NEEDS

MAY 22, 2014

Printed for the use of the Committee on Banking, Housing, and Urban Affairs

Available at: http://www.fdsys.gov/

U.S. GOVERNMENT PRINTING OFFICE

91–224 PDF   WASHINGTON : 2014

(II)

CONTENTS

THURSDAY, MAY 22, 2014

(III)

BRINGING OUR TRANSIT INFRASTRUCTURE TO A STATE OF GOOD REPAIR

THURSDAY, MAY 22, 2014

U.S. Senate,
Subcommittee on Housing, Transportation, and
Community Development,
Committee on Banking, Housing, and Urban Affairs,
Washington, DC.

The Subcommittee met at 9:33 a.m., in room SD–538, Dirksen Senate Office Building, Hon. Robert Menendez, Chairman of the Subcommittee, presiding.

OPENING STATEMENT OF CHAIRMAN ROBERT MENENDEZ

Chairman MENENDEZ. Good morning. This hearing of the Subcommittee on Housing, Transportation, and Community Development is called to order.

Let me thank our witnesses for being here today to discuss what I believe is one of the most important challenges in our Federal transportation program. Investing in our transportation infrastructure and supporting 10 billion passenger trips every year is essential to our mobility, our economic development, our air quality, our overall quality of life, our ability to create jobs, and our global competitiveness. The benefits of investing are clear. The fact is we are not investing enough.

In 2009, a Federal Transit Administration report found that of the seven largest rail systems, including New Jersey Transit, and the systems represented by two of our witnesses today, SEPTA and MBTA, they had a $50 billion backlog in projects—$50 billion just to make sure that the systems were in reasonably good condition, not state-of-the-art but adequate. And, frankly, to me that is simply unacceptable.

Investing in our transit systems is not a luxury. It is a necessity. It is a win-win-win that creates good, family wage jobs. It makes our infrastructure safer, more efficient, more reliable, and it keeps us competitive.

Just recently, my home State of New Jersey received an alarming wakeup call. The president of Amtrak announced that within 20 years, one or both of the tunnels under the Hudson River between New Jersey and New York will need to be shut down. Shutting down the Hudson tunnels is unthinkable, and not investing in keeping them open is unconscionable. These tunnels are over 100 years old, and to make matters worse, they were flooded with corrosive salt water during Hurricane Sandy. Within 20 years these tunnels will be closed unless we commit ourselves to investing in keeping them open.

According to Amtrak, if one of these tunnels were to close, they would have to reduce train traffic from 24 trains an hour to 6 trains per hour. That is four Amtrak trains and two New Jersey Transit trains per hour.

For those of you who are not familiar with the commute from New Jersey into Manhattan, let me tell you that two transit trains an hour is simply not going to cut it. So we go from having the ARC project needlessly canceled, which would have built a new Hudson tunnel and allow for 48 trains per hour, to a future of closed tunnels and 6 trains an hour in the heart of the Northeast corridor. That is simply unthinkable.

Losing the Hudson tunnels is not something our region can work around. There is no detour. There is no extra roadway capacity for the transit and rail commuters to fall back on. We saw it during Sandy when our transit system was inundated. We saw it after 9/11 when people relied on ferry boats to travel to New Jersey from Manhattan. Without a fully functional, multimodal transportation system, the Nation, and New Jersey, is simply stuck in gridlock.

But losing one or both of the Hudson tunnels would mean nothing less than the complete crippling of the region and would send a terrible signal around the world about American competitiveness in the global economy, simply because we are unwilling to make the necessary investments in our transit system.

The Hudson River tunnels are the starkest example of our failure to invest, but every city and town across the country has its own examples. Whether large rail or small bus systems, our transit repair needs total about $86 billion, projected by the DOT to grow to $142 billion by 2030 if we do not begin to invest today.

At the end of the day, we all understand that investing in our infrastructure is not a cheap proposition or politically easy in the current atmosphere. But the cost of inaction is much, much higher.

So I look forward to hearing the perspectives of our witnesses today, and working with my colleagues both on this Committee and as a member of the Finance Committee, we will have to find the funding mechanisms to address these challenges.

Let me introduce the first witness of our first panel. Mr. Dorval Carter is the Chief Counsel for the Federal Transit Administration. In addition to his work at FTA, Mr. Carter previously served in senior positions at the Chicago Transit Authority, a system with a significant state-of-good-repair needs. I look forward to hearing his testimony, which comes with the great depth and breadth of knowledge and perspective of the issue.

Let me say, Mr. Carter, your full statement will be included in the record, without objection. I would ask you to try to summarize it in 5 minutes or so, so we can get into a dialogue. And, with that, the floor is yours.

STATEMENT OF DORVAL CARTER, CHIEF COUNSEL, FEDERAL TRANSIT ADMINISTRATION

Mr. CARTER. Thank you, Chairman Menendez, and thank you for inviting me here today to discuss our Nation's serious deficit in public transportation infrastructure as well as to highlight the

Obama administration's plan to bring our aging rail and bus systems and facilities that support them into a state of good repair as part of the GROW AMERICA Act.

As you stated in your opening remarks, this is a critical time for transit. Transit ridership is at its highest level in generations, and that trend is likely to continue as the U.S. population is expected to increase to approximately 400 million by 2050, while growing proportionally older and more urban.

The caution I bring today is that the foundation we build on to meet that demand is already fracturing. Let us be clear. Transit remains one of the safest ways to travel, but our aging infrastructure carries hidden costs that we cannot and should not ignore.

Our 2013 Conditions and Performance Report finds that the backlog in transit maintenance and replacement stands at $86 billion, a 10-percent increase since 2010. We will need $2.5 billion more every year from all funding sources just to maintain the status quo.

Today it is State and local governments that are bearing the burden, taking on more than half the cost of annual spending to preserve and grow the Nation's transit systems.

The biggest challenge is our rail system, which accounts for about 63 percent of the state-of-good-repair backlog, with most of that due to assets like rail stations, trestles, power substations, and more. These deficiencies have a direct impact on riders. They undermine the resiliency of our transit systems, and they drain resources that could be better spent on timely replacement and expansion.

That is why state of good repair is fundamental to everything that we do at FTA. By providing my testimony here today, you are going to be getting a two-for-one opportunity because not only do I speak for the Administration, but I also speak from the perspective of someone who has worked on the ground with a transit agency to keep transit systems in a state of good repair.

As you indicated, Mr. Chairman, I spent half my career at the Chicago Transit Authority, which operates one of the oldest rail systems in the country. Part of my responsibilities at CTA was managing the capital and operating budgets, the procurement operations, and the warehousing activities of that agency. From that experience, I can tell you that the older a system gets, the more challenging the simplest of tasks become.

For instance, where do you find parts for 100-year-old equipment? No one makes them anymore. You cannot get them off the shelf. Your options are to either cannibalize existing assets or to make the parts yourself. CTA during my tenure had done both. When Hurricane Sandy damaged the equally aged PATH commuter rail system that operates between New Jersey and New York, Chicago was one of the few places that they could turn to for replacement parts.

Let me suggest that we cannot keep transit systems safe and reliable with a Craigslist approach. Instead, we need to make the right investments to get ahead of the problem and keep us there so that we are not always a step behind. That means striking a responsible balance between investing in new capital construction and preserving and modernizing existing infrastructure.

One of the best tools that we have to prioritize these investments is the Transit Asset Management Planning Tool. We are grateful to this Committee for making it a requirement as part of MAP–21. With better metrics and performance-based planning, we can get a more accurate picture of true need, enabling local decision makers to allocate limited resources more effectively systemwide.

We used transit assessment management at CTA, and it was an invaluable tool. It helped us prioritize unmet capital needs and support the argument for public funding. Moreover, it provided a road map so that Federal, State, and local funding partners knew that we had a concrete plan to use our resources efficiently and wisely.

With your help, we are working to bring those benefits to the transit agency nationwide. The latest Condition and Performance Reports make the case for sustained investment and the GROW AMERICA Act answers. The Administration has put forth a plan that builds on the investments made through MAP–21, DOT programs, and the American Recovery and Reinvestment Act to address our infrastructure backlog. The GROW AMERICA Act is the right plan to keep transit safe and reliable now and for future generations.

With that, Mr. Chairman, I conclude my testimony, and I will be happy to answer any questions that you may have.

Chairman MENENDEZ. Well, just to show the efficiency of transit, you did not even use your 5 minutes.

[Laughter.]

Chairman MENENDEZ. Let me start off with one of the critical questions before the Congress, which is the funding level of the transportation reauthorization. And so if Federal funding remains flat in the coming years, do you believe that we can make any progress toward eliminating the $86 billion backlog?

Mr. CARTER. No, sir, I do not. Our Conditions and Performance Report indicated that we need at least an additional $2.5 billion a year from all funding sources just to maintain the existing backlog. In order to make any sort of a dent in that backlog, you are going to need somewhere around the neighborhood of $18.5 billion over a 4-year period to make that happen.

So in order to basically address this problem, we have to make significant additional investments in our transit infrastructure, and the President's proposal is one of the ways in which we believe we can do that.

Chairman MENENDEZ. So flat funding does not only not meet the backlog challenge, I would assume; it will accumulate a greater backlog, a greater cost.

Mr. CARTER. That is correct.

Chairman MENENDEZ. Now, in your testimony you speak to the excellent work that FTA has done for years trying to bring attention to the state-of-good-repair backlog and discuss the importance of the creation of a formula-based state-of-good-repair program under MAP–21. And I agree with your assessment of the importance of this program, but I know some have concerns about the funding increase given in MAP–21 to the state of good repair.

Can you speak to the need for having a strong Federal state-of-good-repair system?

Mr. CARTER. Absolutely. If you look at the overall percentages for the contributions that the Federal Government makes to the issue of state of good repair, we actually only provide about 40 percent of the total contribution. The remaining 60 percent comes from our State and local governmental partners.

It is critical for all of us, both Federal, State, and local, to provide a level of funding that is both reliable and sustainable over an extended period of time in order to address this backlog. The stopping and starting of these types of funds makes it very difficult for transit agencies, both big and small, to properly plan for and to address their capital backlog needs.

Chairman MENENDEZ. Are there certain types of modes or transit systems that are driving the current backlog?

Mr. CARTER. The rail systems make up approximately 60 percent of the backlog. That is primarily due to the heavy cost of their infrastructure. As you can imagine, replacing power substations and rebuilding train stations and things of that nature is a significant cost. But I would not want to diminish the impact that this issue has on the smaller systems as well. As you can imagine, to a small operator in a rural part of the country who may only have two or three buses, if one of those buses is 20 years old and the ability to properly maintain that bus is difficult, resulting in unreliable service, then the impact to that operator is just as significant as the impact of a crumbling infrastructure would be to a Boston, an MBTA, a New York MTA, or a CTA.

Chairman MENENDEZ. Now, you in your testimony you gave an unsettling anecdote, which I know firsthand from my visits with Port Authority officials when the PATH in Hoboken, New Jersey, was inundated, and they were showing me the circuit breakers that are so old that they no longer are manufactured, and you mentioned that they had to resort to shipping in ports from Chicago.

Is that an exception? How pervasive is that type of challenge throughout the system?

Mr. CARTER. Well, I am sure that the other GMs who will speak after me can probably speak to this in more detail than I can, but I can tell you from my experience at CTA, the older transit systems like Chicago, Philadelphia, Boston, and others are dealing with the harsh reality that their infrastructure is extremely old, that replacement parts are difficult to find, and it is only by luck that we are able to identify scenarios like the one that occurred with PATH where there was another system, thankfully, that was able to provide those parts on a temporary basis while PATH went through the process of really having to remanufacture the parts they needed themselves.

Chairman MENENDEZ. Your testimony notes that more people are choosing to live in urban areas where cars are less necessary, younger people less reliant on cars than previous generations. It seems to me those factors are leading to more transit ridership among other elements.

Could these increasing demands on transit systems result in the SGR backlog growing at a faster rate than the $2.5 billion increase per year that you currently project? And is there any modeling that is going on for these changes in calculating the backlog?

Mr. CARTER. Our Condition and Performance Report is based on some modeling that we utilize to forecast what we believe the reasonable growth in transit would be over a period of time. But I think it is safe to say that as demand increases, the backlog is going to become more and more of a problem. Our models suggest that. I think that as we continue to address this problem, we are going to have to deal with the reality of both the challenge of providing an adequate level of funding to maintain the existing systems while dealing with the expansion needs that are required to grow those systems even more.

Chairman MENENDEZ. Finally, asset management, and I think we will hear a little bit more about this from some of our next panel. One of the key changes authorized by this Committee in MAP–21 was the creation of the transit asset management requirement. What work is being done with transit agencies representing different sizes and models to determine best practices and create a standard that works for different types of systems?

Mr. CARTER. We are currently in a rulemaking process that basically is intended to get significant input from the industry as to how we should approach our transit asset management program. We also are in the process of developing technical assistance for agencies to allow them to be in a better position to implement these types of requirements as well as developing additional tools that they will be able to utilize that the Federal Government will provide that will allow them to do the analysis necessary to develop a Transit Asset Management Plan.

We believe that it is critical that we have good, solid industry input into this process and that we develop a process and a program that will address the various capacities and technical capacities of the various size agencies that will have to implement it.

Chairman MENENDEZ. Senator Warren.

Senator WARREN. Mr. Chairman, thank you, and thank you for calling this hearing. I have questions for the next two witnesses, so I will just hold until then.

Chairman MENENDEZ. OK.

Senator WARREN. Thank you.

Chairman MENENDEZ. One final question. Workers' rights. You know, we think about the challenges of transit system's operating systems and facing fiscal challenges in the state-of-good-repair status. I also think your testimony says that nationwide almost a third of the facilities used by local transit agencies to house their operations staff and service their vehicles are in a marginal or poor state of repair.

Are these facilities a threat to the health and welfare of our transit workers?

Mr. CARTER. Well, first, I think I should be clear that we believe the systems are safe. Transit is one of the safest modes of travel that we have available to us in this day and age.

We also believe very strongly that there are steps that need to be taken in order to address the safety not just of the general public but of the employees who work for these agencies as well.

There is no question that when you are dealing with an aging infrastructure and the needs that are required to maintain that infrastructure, employees are going to be working in hazardous conditions with moving vehicles and things of that nature, that can make for an unsafe situation. But there are steps that transit agencies take and do take, and I know from my own experience we focus very closely at CTA on making sure that our operators have appropriate training, the appropriate tools, the appropriate protocols are in place to maximize the safety of those employees when they would engage in these types of activities.

But the reality is that for as long as it is going to take to fix this problem, that will require more workers to work in environments where that could be a more dangerous situation than if it were in a state of good repair.

Chairman MENENDEZ. All right. Well, thank you for your testimony. We look forward to continuing being engaged with you as we develop the legislation that the Committee is considering on the transit side of MAP–21 authorization.

We appreciate your testimony, and you are excused.

Mr. CARTER. Thank you, Mr. Chairman.

Chairman MENENDEZ. Let us now hear from our three transit agencies about their work trying to maintain their systems to a state of good repair. And as I call them up, I want to remind all of our witnesses that their full statements will be included in the record, and we would ask you to summarize your statement within 5 minutes or so, so that we could enter into a dialogue with you.

Our first witness is Mr. Joseph Casey. He is the general manager for the Southeastern Pennsylvania Transportation Authority. SEPTA service is important to a number of my constituents as well, so I appreciate your willingness to appear before the Subcommittee today.

I know that Senator Warren would like to introduce Dr. Beverly Scott, and I think that this moment would be a good time to do so.

Senator WARREN. Thank you very much, Mr. Chairman. It is my great pleasure to introduce Dr. Beverly Scott, who is the general manager at the Massachusetts Bay Transportation Authority, our MBTA, and the administrator for MassDOT rail and transit. Dr. Scott is responsible for managing the MBTA, overseeing the Commonwealth's 15 regional transit authorities, and MassDOT's freight and passenger rail program.

Dr. Scott has tremendous expertise in these issues, not only in Massachusetts but also nationally. Her career in the public transportation industry spans more than three decades and includes executive and senior leadership positions with some of the Nation's largest public transit systems.

Prior to coming to the MBTA, Dr. Scott served as chief executive officer and general manager of the Metropolitan Atlanta Rapid Transit Authority, MARTA, where she was the first woman to hold that position. Additionally, she served as general manager and chief executive officer of the Sacramento Regional Transit District, SRTD, and she also served as the general manager of the Rhode Island Public Transit Authority, RIPTA.

Dr. Scott is nationally recognized for her extraordinary leadership and thoughtful advocacy in advancing increased investment for effective and efficient transit infrastructure. She is a leader in her field and was named Transportation Innovator of Change by President Obama and the U.S. Department of Transportation for

8

her long record of strong leadership and innovation in the transportation industry.

We are very pleased to have you in Massachusetts and very pleased to have you here today in Washington. Thank you.

Ms. SCOTT. Senator, thank you so much.

Chairman MENENDEZ. Thank you, Senator Warren. It sounds like every system could use a doctor.

And, finally, our third witness today is Mr. Gary Thomas, who serves as the president and executive director of the Dallas Area Rapid Transit, so we thank you for joining us.

Mr. Casey, we will start off with you and move down the aisle. As I said, your full statements will be included in the record. Please try to summarize them in about 5 minutes or so, and then we can get into some back and forth.

STATEMENT OF JOSEPH M. CASEY, GENERAL MANAGER, SOUTHEASTERN PENNSYLVANIA TRANSPORTATION AUTHORITY, PHILADELPHIA, PENNSYLVANIA

Mr. CASEY. Good morning. Chairman Menendez, Senator Warren, I want to thank you for the opportunity to testify on the Federal role in bringing this Nation's public transportation infrastructure to a state of good repair. I am Joseph Casey, general manager of the Southeastern Pennsylvania Transportation Authority—SEPTA—located in Philadelphia, Pennsylvania. SEPTA is the sixth largest public transit operator in the country and the largest in Pennsylvania. SEPTA provides 1.2 million daily passenger trips, which are essential in supporting the economy of the southeastern Pennsylvania region.

Last year, Americans took 10.7 billion trips on public transportation, yet at a time when transit ridership reached its highest levels in 57 years, the industry continues to fall behind in the investment required to bring our transit systems to a state of good repair.

According to the 2013 Conditions and Performance Report released by the U.S. Department of Transportation in February, the state-of-good-repair backlog for transit systems nationwide has risen to $86 billion. This number is projected to grow by $2.5 billion per year, and the report states that total spending on state of good repair from all sources must increase by $8.2 billion per year to address this backlog.

The funding and operational pressures related to state of good repair are particularly acute in the large urban transit systems with aging rail infrastructure. Infrastructure related to rail transportation accounts for a significant majority of the national transit state-of-good repair backlog.

SEPTA's experience demonstrates the need for investment and the cost of not investing. Our current backlog of unmet infrastructure needs is now $5 billion—nearly three-quarters of which is concentrated in SEPTA's aging rail infrastructure.

Our challenges are not unique among large, old rail systems. In northeast Illinois, the investment that would be required to bring Chicago's regional rail transit systems to a state of good repair would be roughly $20 billion. In Georgia, the Metropolitan Atlanta Rapid Transit Authority, MARTA, will see their state-of-good-repair backlog grow to $7 billion by 2024 without an additional state- of-good-repair investment.

In MAP–21, the Congress responded to the rail state-of-good-repair crisis by creating a new state-of-good-repair formula grants program and increasing funding for the Nation's rail transit systems to invest in the critical state-of-good-repair needs. On behalf of the transit riders in our region, I want to thank the Committee for this role in making that program a reality.

Since 2010, I have served as Chair of an informal group of the Nation's largest, oldest rail transit systems, the Metropolitan Rail Discussion Group, that together carry approximately 80 percent of the Nation's public transportation passengers. We continue to maintain, as we have since our formation in 2007, that the long-term, predictable, and growing transit program that emphasize state-of-good-repair investment in the rail transit systems that enable this Nation's world-class economies is not just good transit policy but sound economic policy as well.

To understand the entire cost of not investing, we need to look beyond ridership impact to the broader economic benefits of public transit in our major metropolitan areas. These areas rely on public transportation to fuel economic growth and competitiveness by connecting employees to their jobs, allowing freight and vehicle commuters to move on less congested highways, and providing important mobility options for all members of the community.

The Nation's economy is damaged when our major metropolitan areas cease to function efficiently as gateways for the movement of goods and people between U.S. and international destinations. Maintaining the infrastructure that supports metropolitan rail transit systems is an established national priority, and Congress must preserve the Federal Government's 50-year-plus commitment to public transportation and preserve the strength of the mass transit account in the Highway Trust Fund.

We spend too much time focusing on the cost of Government infrastructure programs and too little time focusing on the crippling cost of not investing in infrastructure. A short-term patch on the Highway Trust Fund highway and transit accounts will not address the crucial shortfall in investment. If Congress takes that approach—either for 6 months, a year, or 2 years—transit systems will again be left without the appropriate funding or budget certainty needed to plan and execute major infrastructure rehabilitation projects.

It has been more than 4½ years since the expiration of the last transportation bill that provided any long-term investment and planning ability. The intervening period has been marked with uncertainty and insufficient funding growth. I urge this Subcommittee and the full Committee to develop a plan for a multiyear public transportation investment program with funding levels that increase from year to year to meet the growing needs across the country. A robust and growing rail transit state of good repair and a fully funded core capacity program that allows aging systems to sensibly accommodate ridership growth while continuing to address state-of-good-repair needs should be the centerpieces of the national transit program.

I want to thank you for the opportunity to testify today, and I look forward to answering any questions you may have.

Chairman MENENDEZ. Thank you.

Dr. Scott.

STATEMENT OF BEVERLY A. SCOTT, GENERAL MANAGER AND CHIEF EXECUTIVE OFFICER, MASSACHUSETTS BAY TRANSPORTATION AUTHORITY

Ms. SCOTT. Chairman Menendez, Senator Warren, it is a pleasure to have the opportunity to testify this morning.

For overall context, the Massachusetts Bay Transportation Authority, affectionately called "The T," is the fifth largest public transit provider in the United States with more than 1.3 million passenger trips per day and close to 400 million trips per year, and that is across an extensive heavy light rail, bus, commuter rail, water ferry, and paratransit network.

We are also the oldest major public transit system in the United States with a subway system that opened in 1897, the oldest in the country, which still operates today at crush loads every average weekday peak period, and a commuter rail network that was originally laid out in the 1830s, among some of the first railroads in the country—a network which remains today a vital link for our Commonwealth, our partner States throughout New England and in the Northeast region, and the national passenger rail network along the Northeast corridor.

On our bus side, a critical element of our overall transit network, some of our bus facilities date back to the early 20th century, having been initially designed to serve horse-drawn omnibuses.

As you would expect, achieving a state of good repair is a significant challenge for the T. Today we estimate our backlog of state of good repair at close to $5 billion. It is a challenge that we live every day, our customers experience with us every day, and our employees work to overcome every day.

Speaking of our transit workforce, the people infrastructure—those who plan, design, operate, and maintain our systems, particularly our frontline employees—it is also extremely important that workforce development at all levels is not an afterthought as we grapple with our need to achieve a state of good repair.

All of this said, while we still have a long way to go and definitely need a continued, strong Federal partner, including significantly increased Federal investment in our critical transportation infrastructure, both in our existing and well-supported new targeted transit investments, under the leadership of Governor Patrick we are making strides through implementation of a serious transportation reform agenda, including actions to bring transit employee health care and retirement benefits in line with other State agencies, the implementation of sustainable internal productivity and cost containment measures, and the deployment of new technologies to improve our overall customer experience.

On top of this transportation reform agenda, our Governor proposed the Way Forward transportation program this past year to provide much needed increased local funding for our statewide transportation, a self-help plan, if you will, including the MBTA, and statewide rail and transit, including our 15 regional transit authorities. And this year, this past year, that was successful with the help of our legislature, the business, and our communities across the Commonwealth, resulting this past year in the passage of the largest bond package for transportation as well as significant new investments sustainably for transportation in the Commonwealth's history, including new State revenues dedicated to funding transportation, the first increase in over 20 years of the State gasoline tax, and this increase is aligned with inflation to ensure that the level of funding will keep pace over time.

The reason I say these things is, as we stressed this morning, the absolute criticality of a strong Federal partnership, predictability of funding, and significantly increased Federal funding to help to turn the tide on this. I want to make it very clear that we appreciate and we respect at the local level that we need to step up and do our part as well, and so that is what you see on the part of our Commonwealth.

So what I will say is that things have certainly gotten much better and we are continuing, but we are definitely in great need of continued support by the Federal Government.

On the side of—I want to take a little bit now—state of good repair, fix it first, commonsense must happen. But at the same time we cannot wind up only looking at the hole and not the doughnut, and that means that we have to also make new targeted investments for growth. And so for us, the most notable of those projects at the Federal level is our Green Line expansion project, which we are moving through the New Starts program at this point in time. And this project will, in fact, wind up for us filling what has been a missing transit link serving some of the most densely populated communities, honestly, in the United States. Right now those communities of Somerville, Medford, and Cambridge are only within— only 20 percent of those communities are within distance today of a rail station. When this project—and prayerfully, we will, in fact, hopefully receive an FFGA for this project, when that is over, we will then be able to provide access for what is over 50 percent environmental justice communities for within—75 percent of those communities will be within walking distance to rail, which will significantly wind up decreasing their travel times by 65 to 75 percent and opening up a tremendous vista, if you will, of new job and economic development opportunities for a much needed community.

So at this point, we have done everything—asset management, thank you, Federal Transit Administration, for all of their support. We believe that we are struggling like everybody else but cutting-edge, if you will, in terms of asset management and moving in that direction. Performance metrics, this is how we do our work. We are extremely transparent in terms of what we consider the metrics to be in working with the public. And we have also aligned what we are doing on the transportation side with critical public policies having to do with housing affordability, greening, resilience, just— it is not just transit for transit's sake. It is really about livability, overall economic competitiveness, and the way.

So, in conclusion, as we experience record high and growing transit ridership and increasingly aging systems, reaffirming the Federal commitment in partnership with a program that has both predictability and growth is essential to making real progress to turn the tide on the state-of-good-repair backlog, and this is one that States and localities cannot successfully tackle on our own. Federal partnership and investment is key.

So, with deep respect, thank you very much.

Chairman MENENDEZ. Thank you.

Mr. Thomas.

STATEMENT OF GARY THOMAS, PRESIDENT AND EXECUTIVE DIRECTOR, DALLAS AREA RAPID TRANSIT

Mr. THOMAS. Thank you, Chairman Menendez and Committee Members. I appreciate the opportunity to be here today. My name is Gary Thomas, and I am the president/executive director of Dallas Area Rapid Transit. We have a little bit different story to tell. We are not over 100 years old. As a matter of fact, we are just over 30 years old now. The voters of North Texas voted to dedicate a 1-percent sales tax in 1983 to create a transportation agency, and today we operate bus, light rail, commuter rail, paratransit services, and HOV services in the North Texas region covering a 700-square-mile area, 13 cities, and about 2.4 million people, providing roughly 107 million trips annually. I would also like to add that we operate the longest light-rail system in North America.

So as you can see, we have had very rapid growth, opening our first light-rail segment in 1996, and now operating 85 miles. Later this year we will add an additional 5 miles as we go to DFW Airport. We will open that segment 4½ months early and under budget. While our oldest segments are now only 18 years old, our growth and subsequent state of good repair is closely controlled by a 20-year financial plan that we strictly adhere to.

This financial plan, by policy, ensures that we balance our anticipated revenues against our operational expenses, our asset management, and our capital expansion. Even though we are relatively young, we have over 15 years of asset management experience. One of the biggest key components of our program is a regularly scheduled asset condition assessment that we do on an annual basis, and then once every 5 years, we have an outside consultant come in and verify where we are and then determine if there is a course correction that needs to be made.

The good news is that MAP–21 ensures a more unified approach industry-wide regarding the development of transit asset management plans holding each of us accountable for managing our assets responsibly. We are supportive of allowing the FTA to complete their process and the industry time to implement the new policies before making major policy revisions in a new transportation bill.

The good news, and perhaps the bad news, is that we have created a large appetite for transportation choices in North Texas. This obviously relates to where people live, where they work, and we see that happening, surprisingly, as some people might find, in North Texas every day. This appetite requires not only maintaining our existing system, but growth of the system to address the fourth largest and one of the fastest growing metropolitan regions in the country. Over 73 percent of our capital expenditures for the next 20 years is for SGR, leaving very little for growth, even though the demand is great.

13

One of our key areas of need addressing both SGR and growth is what is happening in our core area of our system. Right now we have a hub-and-spoke system, and the hub is a single corridor through downtown Dallas. Because of the growth of the system and the service that we provide and the growth of that service, the track conditions in the corridor are deteriorating faster than we initially anticipated. This means that we will start a $45 million capital program later this summer, replacing over the next couple of years the rail through this core area. Additionally, we are planning a core capacity set, or group of projects, to relieve the pressure on this existing core. Therefore, we are a strong advocate for the core capacity program initiated in MAP–21 to be preserved in the next surface transportation bill. Our core capacity project as envisioned provides capacity and flexibility while reducing maintenance needs in the future. So a lot of the new starts and new projects actually go hand in hand with the core capacity as well as state-of-good-repair projects.

Mr. Chairman, in conclusion, in order to continue to provide transportation choices for North Texas, we desperately need a long-term, fully funded transportation bill providing stability and predictability for our agency and, more importantly, for our customers. We applaud the 6-year term in the proposed highway bill and the funding levels in the GROW AMERICA legislation. I would hope that this Committee would consider both of those and consider the APTA recommendation and merge these two together, resulting in a 6-year fully funded bill for transit of $104 billion.

Of course, where public transit goes, community grows, and on behalf of our board of directors, our 3,700 employees, and our millions of customers, thank you for this opportunity today, and I look forward to answering any questions.

Chairman MENENDEZ. Thank you all for your testimony.

Let me first start with maybe a couple of yeses or noes, if we can. DOT's Conditions and Performance Report tells us that if recent investment levels are maintained, by the year 2030, which is only 16 short years from now, the Nation's transit system will be facing $142 billion in deferred system preservation—I underline "preservation"—projects. Given that Federal funding makes up more than a quarter of the investments, it seems that we have work to do.

Just by a simple yes or no, does anyone on the panel believe the current funding levels are enough to help you achieve a state of good repair? We will start off with you, Mr. Casey. If you would put your microphones on while we are doing this, I would appreciate it, for the record.

Mr. CASEY. They are insufficient.

Chairman MENENDEZ. Dr. Scott.

Ms. SCOTT. Woefully insufficient.

Chairman MENENDEZ. Mr. Thomas.

Mr. THOMAS. No, sir.

Chairman MENENDEZ. OK. And if Federal funding remains flat, does anyone believe—or is it a possibility—and I have heard, Dr. Scott, your testimony about the Commonwealth. But does anyone believe if we just remain flat that additional State and local funding alone can cover the cost of starting to pay down the backlog? Mr. Casey.

Mr. CASEY. No. I will say that last year the Pennsylvania Commonwealth passed a transportation bill. It was approximately half of what our needs are going forward to address our state of good repair. So, no, the State actually did their share, I think, but I think the Federal Government really needs to step up and do a similar bill.

Chairman MENENDEZ. Dr. Scott.

Ms. SCOTT. Same, sir. Not possible.

Chairman MENENDEZ. Mr. Thomas.

Mr. THOMAS. While we have a large local match with our 1-percent sales tax, it is not nearly enough to do what we need to do as we move forward.

Chairman MENENDEZ. Now, Mr. Casey, your testimony states that the state-of-good-repair challenges are particularly acute for large urban rail systems, and you noted that the average age of SEPTA's rail bridges is more than 80 years old, 103 bridges that are more than 100 years old. That is a pretty challenging reality for the system.

What practical impact do these needs have on your riders on a day-to-day basis?

Mr. CASEY. Well, we were faced with shutting down a lot of our rail system prior to the transportation bill out of Harrisburg. From a practical standpoint, your first issue is slow orders, you slow down the track, and then you have weight restrictions, and then eventually shutting down the structure.

We have with the funding that we received from the State—prior to the funding from the State, we had no bridge repairs in our capital program. Now that we did get State funding, I have 18 bridges that I am addressing in the next 5 years. And just to give you the age of some of these bridges, I will go through—there are 18 of them. The construction was 1891, 1900, 1891, 1900, 1896, 1916; a major bridge was built in 1895, and it is significant because it spans 922 feet, 150 feet in the air off the ground. I could go on and on. I have bridges here, 1876, 1854, 1834, 1834, 1906, et cetera.

We have a very old system, and a lot of this was built, you know, Penn Central, the Reading Railroad, et cetera, that all went bankrupt. Very little has been done to repair these, to replace these structures.

We were in dire straits. The State funding gave us the ability to help dig out of this hole, but as I said, with over 103 bridges over 100 years old, you know, we can only address 18 of them in the next 5 years.

Chairman MENENDEZ. Dr. Scott, you said something—maybe it is not about bridges in the T's case, but you talked about how your passengers also face the challenges with you. What are some of those challenges?

Ms. SCOTT. Same types of things: slow orders, just an inability to be able——

Chairman MENENDEZ. For the record, for those who may read it and not know what a slow order is.

Ms. SCOTT. A slow order means that there will be a period along a stretch of the track where simply because of the condition—it could be a bridge or a tunnel segment or whatever—I have got to really—instead of being able to take it at the speeds that it really could go through from a science standpoint, we have got to slow it down. Sometimes you are talking taking it to a crawl of 5 to 10 miles per hour, which means—you can imagine what that means in terms of the commute time for our riders. And so it is—and you ultimately get to the point where you just have to—you just literally have to close down a segment.

Chairman MENENDEZ. Let me ask you, Mr. Thomas, your testimony notes that DART is considering applying to the new core capacity program within the New Starts account. And I think there is often a perception that the program is used primarily by much older, heavier rail systems. Can you talk about the importance of a Federal core capacity program in helping a newer light-rail system like DART maintaining a state of good repair?

Mr. THOMAS. Yes, sir. The core capacity program in our particular case would be incredibly vital and important as we continue to expand our system. We are really at a point now where, if we add to our system, we cannot get more trains through the single corridor that goes through our downtown area. So before we can add any more to our system, or really, as I tell a lot of folks locally, if something happens on the corridor—a fire happened on that corridor not too long ago. The fire department put their hoses across the corridor. They did not appreciate the idea of us rolling trains across that fire hose. So we had to actually stop service during rush hour to make sure that we dealt with it. So the core capacity program gives us the flexibility and it gives us the capacity to do that.

Now, what we are looking at, Mr. Chairman, is a combination of projects, understanding that, on the one hand, we have got to provide our local match; on the other hand, the core capacity program is limited in size right now. So we are looking at how we can reduce the size of the project and maybe combine projects to deal with that capacity issue in our downtown area. Currently we are looking at replacing the rail in the downtown area. Because of the traffic, and the amount of traffic that we have put through downtown, the trains have already worn through the hardened surface on the rail, and so it is eating through the rest of the steel very, very quickly.

So we are at a point now where we have got to replace that to maintain our SGR and at the same time figure out how to expand the system to give us the flexibility and capacity through downtown that we need. So that program ends up being critically important to us as we move forward.

Chairman MENENDEZ. I have a couple other key questions, but I want to turn to my colleague. Senator Merkley.

Senator MERKLEY. Thank you very much, Mr. Chairman, and thank you to all of you.

I want to ask just a limited question that has come from several of my transit districts, so given your experience on the ground, I thought you might have some insight on this. This is essentially the situation where the discretionary grants have been changed to a funding formula in the bus and bus facility program under MAP–21. And the result for a couple of my transit districts is they are having a great difficulty acquiring replacement buses in the fashion that they did before, which means they are buying fewer, therefore not getting group bus discounts, and they are keeping inefficient buses that need high levels of maintenance on routes for longer to the detriment of the agency.

Have you all experienced in your own respective realms any challenge like this? I would invite any of you to answer.

Mr. CASEY. I have not, no.

Senator MERKLEY. OK.

Ms. SCOTT. I have not at the T, but we have 15 regional transit authorities which are much smaller systems, and while we keep a good overview from the broad Commonwealth level, I can tell you that it is more challenging for them.

Senator MERKLEY. Thank you.

Mr. THOMAS. Yes, sir. From our perspective, again, I have not, and I think it really relates to the size of the agency and the wherewithal and the forward planning. And the larger agencies, in many cases they can accommodate that. And the smaller agencies, quite frankly, they cannot. And the trickle of money does not buy a bus, and you cannot save it up that quickly.

Senator MERKLEY. Well, thank you for sharing that directly from the front line, and I am listening in with interest through the questions my colleagues are asking, and I am going to pass this on. Thank you.

Chairman MENENDEZ. Senator Warren.

Senator WARREN. Thank you, Mr. Chairman, Senator Merkley.

I would like to ask a question from a little different direction, and that is about the economic impact of our transportation infrastructure and the state of our transportation infrastructure. As I see it, the economy turns on transportation infrastructure. This is how people get to work. This is how businesses get their goods to market. And without a transportation infrastructure or with a decaying transportation infrastructure, the whole economy is in trouble.

So, Dr. Scott, you mentioned the Green Line extension, and I would like for just a minute to talk about that. This is an extension of the T that would go to one of the most densely populated areas in the country, principally to Somerville, Massachusetts. I was very pleased to see that the President had included $100 million in his fiscal year 2015 budget in order to get this expansion of the T. But what I would like to do is start with this question, Dr. Scott: Can you talk about what the lack of basic infrastructure has done to the economy of Somerville? And then we will talk about the other side.

Ms. SCOTT. I would tell you that what it has done is that it has stymied it. From one standpoint, just let me talk about the jobs portion of it. It has made it much more difficult for people within the Somerville area to, in fact, be able to access good employment opportunities. And so that is, both outside as well as development within Somerville, it has made it much more difficult for Somerville to be able to attract employment and business opportunities.

Now, what I can say to you is that I just always look at things are what they are, and so just with the knowledge that this project is coming—and we are absolutely committed to this project. Just look at the development that has started to take place already. You go and, in fact, we—and we were delighted that Secretary Foxx actually took a little time to come through to actually see the project.

At NorthPoint, right there where we have Lechmere, 2.2 million in terms of development, office, residential, multi-use. At Union Square, another 2 million square feet of development. This is development that absolutely would not be taking place; they are both absolutely right there where the transit is—literally, at the Union Square, the station is actually right there where the development is. And then you look at what is taking place at places like MaxPak.

So the growth and the development that is just being catalyzed, if you will, by that Green Line expansion project are just—it is just absolutely unbelievable.

Senator WARREN. Well, I have walked through and seen this, and it really is terrific. I was going to ask you the other half, and that is, you know, it is expensive up front to make these investments, and yet study after study shows that when we do, we get enormous economic impact. We get job growth. We get economic development. So I want to thank you. And I want to thank you for your advocacy on behalf of the Green Line, but also your advocacy on behalf of the whole transit system. Enormously valuable.

Ms. SCOTT. Thank you. Thank you. But, you know, just—the American Public Transportation Association at the gross level has done work on this. For every $1 that winds up going into transit, the multiplier effect in terms of four—at least $4 that wind up coming in terms of what we call that broader impact, and then not just in terms of property values and residential development and all of that, but then looking at it as well in terms of jobs creation. I have seen numbers that have been—for every $1 billion, we are looking at something like about 32,000 to 40,000 jobs that wind up being created.

So it is the engine. I always laugh and tell people that it is not the infrastructure that is the ''it.'' It is actually the outcomes and the benefits that we have for people in communities.

Senator WARREN. Yes. And, actually, let me just extend that over to Dallas, because I have been looking at the studies there as well. You know, you have had amazing growth, gone from zero hard rail to miles and miles of a system in 30 years. And I saw two recent studies by the University of North Texas that estimated that the $4.7 billion spent between 2002 and 2013 to expand light rail in the Dallas system has already generated over $7.4 billion in regional economic activity, including tens of thousands of jobs that paid in excess of $3.3 billion in salaries, wages, and benefits; and made the point also in one of these studies that more than 5.3 billion in private capital transit-oriented development projects have been built or are under construction or are planned near the DART light-rail stations.

So we are over time, but if Mr. Chairman will indulge me for just a minute, I wanted to give you a chance, Mr. Thomas, to talk about, based on your experience, how capital investment in rail transit can stimulate economic growth and whether or not your experience in Dallas can be replicated in other places around the country.

Mr. THOMAS. You know, it has been fascinating to watch, Senator, what has happened in Dallas, because when we first started, we were focused on getting the rail on the line obviously to move people safely, efficiently, and effectively. There were other people that understood the value of that infrastructure, the value that they could take advantage of, quite frankly, and take advantage of in a good way for our community. And once that started, once people started realizing, now as we look to other areas in the expansion, it is certainly to move people, but it is also the air quality opportunities, the congestion mitigation opportunities, and then the economic development opportunities.

There was a point in time when the economy got a little soft and we had to start talking about a delay. We literally had buses of people showing up at our board meetings to explain to us why that was not a good idea to delay those projects. And in large part, it was due to not just the transportation but the economic development opportunities that had already been thought about and already planned. As you mentioned, the study that was recently completed by the University of North Texas was an update of a study that had been done previously, and that was a very, very narrowly tailored study because it only looked at projects that were on the tax rolls. So publicly funded projects, the big hospital expansion, the new Civic Center, those were not even on that list. And so it is pretty incredible to see not only the projects of economic development, but also the rental rates is part of that study, and it shows the increase in rental rates within a quarter mile of the station. We are seeing it over and over, proving out the 4:1 benefits that the APTA study has also shown.

Senator WARREN. Thank you. Thank you, Mr. Thomas.

Mr. Chairman, would it be all right to ask Mr. Casey to weigh in from SEPTA's perspective?

Chairman MENENDEZ. Absolutely.

Senator WARREN. Mr. Casey.

Mr. CASEY. We have a very old system, and, unfortunately, the last number of years we have not done a lot of expansion. But what we are seeing is a lot of investors wanting to build facilities, whether it is homes, you know, apartment buildings, et cetera, around our stations and utilizing the benefits of transit for further development because it makes it much more attractive.

But, again, there is a lot of interest in us expanding the system. There is one particular project, we have a Broad Street line, one of our heaviest lines, wants to extend into the former Navy Yard, which is attracting companies from all over the place. So there is an expansion.

But I just want to say that more and more people in Philadelphia are opting or wanting to take public transit. In the last 15 years, we have had a 50-percent growth on the regional rail system—50 percent. And the only thing really limiting us from even further expansion is capacity. The number of vehicles that we have on the regional rail is—has not increased—it actually has increased a little bit, but it is minor. Those cars are already filled up. But it is parking, it is—you know, if I was able to invest, there is no question in my mind you would see easily a double-digit growth in the utilization of those services.

Senator WARREN. Well, I want to thank you all very much.

Thank you for your indulgence, Mr. Chairman. And I just want to say I think Dr. Scott makes exactly the right point. Transportation infrastructure is powerfully important, but not as an end in itself. It is powerfully important because this is how we help our economy move forward.

Thank you, Mr. Chairman.

Chairman MENENDEZ. Thank you.

Just one last set of questions for the panel. If you were sitting here instead of there and being able to write the new transit provisions of MAP–21 outside of the funding issue, which I think we collectively agree on, is there anything that you would change or add that does not exist in the law today?

Mr. CASEY. As far as I am concerned, I just think the—we just need to invest more money into the transit, and whether it is—we have issues from the older properties, but the smaller operators with buses also have issues. The pot just really has to grow. It has been insufficient for us to maintain our current system.

Ms. SCOTT. What I would stress is that—and we have begun to see the threads of it, but I think that a focus in terms of performance and not rewarding bad behavior. I think that that is important. I think that the connecting of the dots of state of good repair with things like going for full funding grant agreements, I think that the more that we do those kinds of things that are self-reinforcing.

I am a person who, when people ask me, "Bev, what are the things that keep you up at night?" I am going to come back to workforce, OK, making sure that there is funding, intentional funding, to help in terms of the workforce development. We put less than probably 0.5 of a percent in terms of training and development of our people, the kinds of things that keep me up at night, and I can assure you, every one of the operators that is here are the issues in terms of we are not going to have excellence in terms of the systems without the people.

Now, I do not want to overdo this, but this is—we have 6,200 employees at the T. I can tell you today that there are 800 folks who have the time and the years to be able to retire. Over 30 percent of those are in my specialized maintenance areas. When I take that number 5 years from now, it becomes 1,800 people who will have the time and the years to be able to retire; 38 percent of them are in my specialized maintenance areas—signal, track, rail controllers. You can replace a general manager faster than we are going to be able to do that. So to see some synergies between this bill and education, workforce and labor, would be absolutely unbelievable.

Chairman MENENDEZ. Mr. Thomas, do you have anything to add?

Mr. THOMAS. Yes, Mr. Chairman. I think it is flexibility. As we have seen this morning, each one of our cities is different. Each city across the country is different. We all have different needs. We are all in different places. And so making sure that the bill going forward offers the flexibility to each of us to do what we need to do in our respective cities to grow the economy, to provide opportunities to people, I think that is critical moving forward.

Chairman MENENDEZ. I appreciate those answers.

Mr. Casey, let me ask you, you chair the Metropolitan Rail Discussion Group, and one of the group's principles is that funding should be prioritized according to need and national importance. To what extent do current Federal programs adhere to that principle? And what changes would you make in that line, if any?

Mr. CASEY. Well, I think it is a recognition of the older systems, and I think when you look at our system and, you know, our needs, you know, in Philadelphia with the number of bridges, and I think people are shocked to learn that we are responsible for 350 bridges, and I think those infrastructure needs are different than—you know, I hate to say maybe Dallas might not have those infrastructure needs. So I think those issues have to be part of the discussions.

You know, one thing I did not discuss is our substation, power substations that are, you know, dealing with 1920 technology that is out there. They have been in operation since, in some cases, the 1920s, 1930s. And generally they are 40, 50 years past their useful life. Those critical issues really need to be addressed as we go forward. And it is not just one of two of them. I mean, I have 15 of the substations that really have to be addressed at one time. And if I have a failure on that, I just cannot—I cannot get the parts. If I fail, it fails, and it is down for a long time.

Chairman MENENDEZ. Dr. Scott, my understanding is that the MBTA has been working to develop an asset management plan for a number of years, well before any Federal requirements were created in MAP–21. Can you give the Committee some details on how your asset management system works? And has it helped you agency better target its investments? And by any chance has the FTA asked you or talked about some best practices that can be considered in new Federal asset management requirements?

Ms. SCOTT. Absolutely. First, I do want to—FTA has been right there at the table with us from the very beginning, and we were some of the first pilot programs that they really helped to fund in terms of being able to develop the data bases and things of that nature.

What I will tell you is that it has radically reshaped—I will be quite candid in terms of how we have done our capital plan, our capital planning. It is no longer—I mean, this is really a robust involvement on the part of all the departments. You have to be very, very clear in terms of exactly what is the need, what is going to wind up being the benefit that winds up coming from it. We are beginning now to—particularly as we bring our maintenance management systems, we are beginning to actually move into being able to look at life cycle so that we can, in fact, actually change the method in terms of how we do procurements. You have to have the data to be able to support being able to do much more in terms of life cycle procurements.

So no capital project comes to the table without there being a full look in terms of not only the aspects of safety and obsolescence, but innovation, resilience, accessibility, and also the people implications and the long-term operating implications of those investments. None of that would have happened if we had not been much more thoughtfully and intentionally looking at both the data as well as just changing our decision lens, if you will, in terms of how we do resource allocation.

It is a work in progress, but very, very different than what we had done in prior years.

Chairman MENENDEZ. Mr. Thomas, you state that DART's capital program has mechanisms built in to deal with funding volatility. Given years of trust fund instability, the uncertainty of the annual appropriations process on the transit New Starts account, and even in the past the Government shutdown, how has the volatility impacted DART's ability to provide reliable transit service? And how are you preparing for the possible concerns as it relates to the Highway Trust Fund?

Mr. THOMAS. Well, certainly as I said, we have a 20-year financial plan, and that 20-year financial plan anticipates all the revenues and all the expenses over the next 20 years. We adjust that annually. Obviously, we do not know exactly what is going to happen for the next 20 years, but we have several economists that work with us to help us identify what is going to happen from a local funding perspective. And then we take a very conservative approach from the Federal participation.

However, if the trust fund is not funded into this calendar year, then it would require us to make significant cuts as we move forward. We are already in the process of looking at what that would be, what those service impacts would be, and starting to determine where that list is and to communicate what that list might look like to our constituents in the North Texas area.

Chairman MENENDEZ. Let me ask you all one final question. I do not know if Senator Warren has any others. But, you know, I assume that in some shape or form you survey or deal with your ridership in trying to understand both their views of operations of your present systems, the views that they may have about any potential expansion or curtailment. So if I were to ask you, switching my role from this position to sitting on the Senate Finance Committee, which has to find a way to fund this, would your ridership support an increase in a revenue source if it is dedicated to the transit system? What would they say?

Mr. CASEY. I would say yes. I think the bottom line, our riders want improved service. They want more frequent service. They want better facilities. And in the region, I think as happened in the State of Pennsylvania, at least our region was almost unanimous in supporting a transportation bill. And I really think the riders and the citizens of that region would support the same.

Chairman MENENDEZ. Dr. Scott.

Ms. SCOTT. I absolutely believe that our public would. I think that there are two pieces to that, however. I think that they will support, but they have to be very clear about what the outcomes are that are intended, and it is about much more than ridership, OK?

And the other is I believe—and I just think that people want accountability, OK? And so the issue, the focus in terms of performance and transparency, but absolutely tied to outcomes that they can be real clear about they want, OK, and with real good transparency and accountability I believe it—and I have another one I would like to just—I forgot to say, and that is that I—you asked the question. I think that at the Federal level, to make sure that every dollar that we do—and you can force this, OK—is to make sure that we make smart investments. So for every dollar, let us make it be a smart dollar, and so that means that everything we can do in terms of technology we need to be looking at, and also what we can do in terms of resilience.

Along our corridor, anything that we do, I tell—this is in the capital program. The water tables are changing. Don't you bring me stuff that was built for 100 years ago, OK? We have to be looking for the future, and so those are, once again, themes in terms of outcomes that you can drive at the Federal level to make every investment we make smart, and also that means that on the research and development end, we are woefully behind in this country, and making investments, because there have been slashes in our research and development funding for transportation, and it is sorely, sorely needed.

Chairman MENENDEZ. Mr. Thomas.

Mr. THOMAS. The voters within our service area certainly have proven over the years that they are supportive of transit and dedicated funding. When they initially voted to approve a 1-percent sales tax in 1983 to create an organization that at the time they had no idea what it would do or what it would be capable of doing, and then subsequently have voted by large margins to allow us to issue long-term debt and other opportunities. So, yes, sir, I believe so.

Chairman MENENDEZ. Senator Warren.

Senator WARREN. No. Thank you.

Chairman MENENDEZ. Well, let me take advantage of one final. I promise this will be the final.

You know, we have a debate in the Committee as it relates to gas tax dollars, which the advocates for highway—and, of course, we are always going to have highways as part of our overall system. But they say, well, a gas tax dollar should not be used for a transit purpose because, you know, it is the drivers who pay the gas tax who ultimately are funding transit systems. Increasingly, however, we have been seeing general fund dollars be used in this respect for funding the overall transportation bill. And it seems to me that as we use more general fund dollars, that argument is increasingly dissipated at the end of the day because general fund dollars are paid by everybody.

So any perspectives on that? I do not know how you deal with it in your respective States.

Mr. CASEY. Well, I have two comments. The vast majority of our riders also drive automobiles, and they are paying the tax also. But the investment in transit——

Chairman MENENDEZ. So they take the transit, let us say, to go to work, but then they have their car for——

Mr. CASEY. Or they drive to the parking lot and then take the train coming in. But the vast majority of the people that still use, benefit from transit, from a congestion standpoint, getting riders off the road, it works hand in hand. And I can tell you there is not sufficient highways within Philadelphia currently to handle all the automobile traffic. Without transit, you know, it would be literally a parking lot.

So the transit benefits everyone, everyone in the region, whether it is the people riding transit or the people on the highways.

Chairman MENENDEZ. But that would have its own economic consequence. If you end in a parking lot, you are not getting your sales force to their sales; you are not getting your workers to work on time, and so many other iterations.

Does anybody else want to comment on this last question?

Ms. SCOTT. I would just say, "Ditto." I tell them, I say, "Get out of that old thinking," OK? All this silo and this is a road dollar and this is a transit dollar and this is a ped dollar. We are all talking about mobility and access. Nothing is free. Everybody—and we are also integrated and interconnected that I just think that that is totally old thinking and that we just need to step it up and move it up and not disregard it, but do not get stuck in it.

Chairman MENENDEZ. Well, we may have you visit some of our colleagues.

[Laughter.]

Chairman MENENDEZ. You might want to think about how you answer in that regard. Mr. Thomas.

Mr. THOMAS. Some of our strongest partners in North Texas are TxDOT and North Texas Tollway Authority, understanding, as Mr. Casey said, it is a collaborative opportunity.

Ms. SCOTT. It is, absolutely.

Chairman MENENDEZ. Well, let me thank all of our witnesses for appearing before the Committee. It is very helpful in developing record, and some of the issues that will undoubtedly be debated among Members, I think the testimony makes a powerful case for the need for strong investments to bring our transit system to a state of good repair. I look forward to working with all of you and others to develop a transit title that can begin to meet some of these needs for the next surface transportation bill.

This record is going to remain open until a week from today if any Senators wish to submit questions for the record. We would ask our witnesses, if you do receive questions, to please respond to them as expeditiously as possible. They are helpful in dealing with some of the questions that we have.

With that, this hearing is adjourned.

[Whereupon, at 10:48 a.m., the hearing was adjourned.]

[Prepared statements and additional material supplied for the record follow:]

PREPARED STATEMENT OF DORVAL CARTER

CHIEF COUNSEL, FEDERAL TRANSIT ADMINISTRATION

MAY 22, 2014

Chairman Menendez, Ranking Member Moran, and Members of the Subcommittee, thank you for inviting me here today to discuss the urgent need to address our Nation's serious public transportation infrastructure deficit and to highlight the Obama administration's plan to bring our aging rail and bus systems and facilities into a state of good repair as part of the GROW AMERICA Act. Transit ridership is at its highest level in generations—exceeding 10 billion trips annually for 7 years in a row. This trend is likely to continue, as the United States' population increases up to an estimated 400 million people by 2050; as a large segment of aging Americans seek to remain independent and mobile without the use of a car; as more people choose to settle in urbanized areas where private automobiles are less necessary; and as younger Americans continue to generally spend less time behind the wheel and more time taking public transportation.

It is absolutely essential for our Nation to invest in safe, modern, reliable, efficient, and affordable public transportation networks that tens of millions of Americans increasingly depend on every day to reach jobs and job training, education, health care, and other opportunities. This means striking a responsible balance between investing in new capital transit construction while also preserving and modernizing existing infrastructure—portions of which were built over a century or more ago—and which continues to serve the public on a daily basis.

On the preservation side of this ledger, we have clearly documented an urgent need to address a transit maintenance and replacement backlog that stands conservatively at $86 billion (in 2010 dollars)—10 percent higher since the Federal Transit Administration (FTA) and the Federal Highway Administration (FHWA) last reported in March 2012 (using 2008 data). This backlog is expected to grow by $2.5 billion each year—unless we make the investments now to slow or stop the growing maintenance deficit. This updated backlog is based on an analysis conducted for the 2013 Status of the Nation's Highways, Bridges and Transit: Conditions and Performance (known as the C&P report), issued jointly by FTA and FHWA in February, 2014.

While transit remains one of the safest ways to travel, the Nation's aging transit infrastructure carries hidden costs that we cannot and should not ignore. Aging transit assets compromise system resiliency. In the wake of Hurricane Sandy, for example, the damaged PATH commuter rail system, which operates critical service between New York and New Jersey, had to replace antiquated circuit breakers and other parts that are no longer manufactured, in order to restore service between Journal Square and Newark Penn Station. PATH literally had to truck in parts from the Chicago Transit Authority—which also uses comparably aged parts in its system. This example serves to illustrate that there are significant costs to maintaining equipment that has exceeded its useful life, with sacrifices made in flexibility, fuel efficiency, and reliability.

Above all, the transit industry's serious deferred maintenance and replacement backlog directly affects average transit riders every day—including transit systems in States represented by Members of this Subcommittee. For example:

- In New Jersey, roughly a third of countywide community transit vehicles (over 300 vehicles) have each logged at least 175,000 miles—a point at which repair bills mount and breakdowns occur more frequently.
- In downstate Illinois, nearly 600 buses and paratransit vehicles that serve riders with disabilities are operating well past their recommended retirement date.
- In West Virginia, 11 locally operating transit systems rely on vehicles that exceed FTA's recommended retirement date, with more than half the vehicles in two of these agencies in this condition, and the others well on the way.
- In State College, Pennsylvania, if funding is not secured to replace 66 buses running on compressed natural gas (CNG) that have exceeded the FTA-recommended retirement date (many of them upwards of 18 years old), then the Centre Area Transportation Authority will need to install new CNG tanks that cost more than the value of these aging buses.
- In Kansas, the City of Paola provides nearly 45,000 rides per year on a single 10-year-old bus, while in Ottaway County, 10,400 passengers annually depend on two buses that are each more than 14 years old.
- In Cleveland, Ohio, 100 percent of the Greater Cleveland Regional Transit Authority's heavy rail vehicles are 30 years old. And in Butler County, Ohio, the local Regional Transit Authority is cannibalizing broken buses for parts to

keep a small fleet of buses operating—in the face of rising demand for bus service.

- In Oakland, California, nearly a quarter of the transit buses are 14 years old—past FTA's recommended retirement date.
- Nationwide, about 28 percent of the facilities used by local transit agencies to house their operations staff and service their vehicles are in a marginal or poor state of repair. Inadequate capital funding to replace this type of infrastructure affects maintenance efficiency and the welfare of the workforce.

In these States, and many more, millions of transit dependent senior citizens, veterans, individuals with disabilities, and others take transit to work and school, and to seek the services and care they require on a daily basis—and as those transit vehicles age, their dependability decreases and gaps in service grow larger, leaving many riders stranded, unable to reach the doctor's office or the grocery store. For riders who take transit by choice, transit systems thrive when they are able to offer a convenient and reliable alternative to driving to work and other destinations. Maintaining and preserving these systems is critical to ensuring they live up to their potential to serve their communities and meet the needs of future riders.

We recognize that the Senate Banking Committee has generally been responsive to FTA's needs for adequate resources to help capitalize the construction of the Nation's transit assets. It is important to bear in mind, nevertheless, that the transit industry's marginal or poor infrastructure condition exists today despite FTA's ongoing financial support of rehabilitation and replacement activities, primarily through the former Section 5309 Fixed Guideway Modernization funds (replaced under MAP–21 with State of Good Repair Formula Grants) and Section 5307 Urbanized Area Formula Grant funds. Yet the scope of the infrastructure deficit persists, and additional resources are needed to address the challenge in a meaningful way. Consider, for example, Chicago's transit environment. Chicago's transit systems (CTA, Metra, and Pace) received about $2.2 billion in Federal funding from FY2009 to FY2013, largely through the above-mentioned FTA programs. These operators also received about $242 million from the American Recovery and Reinvestment Act of 2009 (ARRA) (Pub.L. 111-5), which helped to replace buses and conduct overdue preventive maintenance and subway rehabilitation. Despite this level of investment from multiple sources, according to CTA, these transit systems collectively face a $24 billion backlog over 10 years, requiring a sustained annual investment of $2 billion to address the need.

We believe the data in the latest C&P Report makes a clear case for a sustained, and sustainable, investment plan to address the deteriorating condition of our Nation's transit assets and ensure the safety and viability of public transportation nationwide for future generations.

FTA's Consistent Call for Transit Asset Improvements

It was before this Subcommittee almost 5 years ago, in August 2009, that Federal Transit Administrator Peter Rogoff testified on the need for public transit agencies to achieve and maintain a state of good repair in order to provide safe and reliable service to tens of millions of daily riders.

At that time, FTA pledged to make transit infrastructure repair a policy priority and a key component of the agency's annual budget request. FTA's initial state-of-good-repair initiative included encouraging the industry to share ideas on recapitalization and maintenance; asset management practices; and innovative financing strategies. Over the course of 2008 and 2009, FTA formed a working group with the transit industry, convened a state-of-good-repair roundtable, and published a seminal Rail Modernization Study in 2009 in response to the conference report accompanying the FY2008 Transportation-HUD Appropriations Act and at the request of a dozen senators. That initial study found that more than one-third of the assets at the seven major rail transit systems analyzed (Chicago's CTA, Boston's MBTA, New York's MTA, New Jersey Transit, San Francisco's Bay Area Rapid Transit System, Philadelphia's SEPTA system, and Washington, DC's WMATA system) were in marginal or poor condition. Many of these systems' assets were near or had exceeded their expected useful life and collectively faced an estimated $50 billion maintenance and repair backlog. Given that these systems account for about 80 percent of the Nation's rail transit ridership, the need for action was clear. An expanded version of the study released in 2010 estimated the cost of bringing all of the Nation's rail and bus transit systems into a state of good repair at $77.7 billion—a snapshot in time that further confirmed that serious, targeted investments in this deteriorating infrastructure had to be made as soon as possible. Though the numbers differ slightly, this estimated need is consistent with the C&P Report's estimate—different numbers, same story.

FTA's Rail Modernization Study also found the transit industry's asset management practices were far weaker than they should be. Practices such as the use of decision support tools that rank and prioritize reinvestment needs, and conducting comprehensive asset condition assessments, were largely absent from the industry's regular strategic planning processes.

Every year since the release of these assessments quantifying the Nation's transit state-of-good-repair needs, FTA has worked diligently to help transit agencies improve their transit asset management practices—which is integral to keeping transit safe—and to make a clear case for additional resources for state-of-good-repair needs through the annual appropriations process. Our success culminated in the inclusion of FTA's first formula-based State of Good Repair (SGR) Formula Grant Program as part of the Moving Ahead for Progress in the 21st Century (MAP–21) Act, which is set to expire on September 30, 2014. This program was an important step forward because it provided for the first time 2 years of predictable funding to help transit agencies replace and rehabilitate existing assets or undertake capital projects required to maintain their systems in a state of good repair. The SGR formula program under MAP–21 grew by over $500 million compared to the former fixed guideway modernization program. On the other hand, funding for bus and bus facility replacement and repair went from $984 million under SAFETEA–LU to $428 million in MAP–21, which caused a devastating blow to transit providers' ability to replace aging buses and rehabilitate facilities because of a lack of funds.

FTA's Current Activities To Improve the State of Good Repair of Transit Infrastructure

Under MAP–21, transit agencies are required to develop a transit asset management plan to help them strike a better and more informed balance between preservation and expansion needs—in the context of a safety-first performance culture. To this end, FTA is actively implementing a new National Transit Asset Management System through the rulemaking process, supplemented by technical assistance and outreach to grantees. This approach represents an innovative and important step toward helping the transit industry to obtain better metrics, through performance-based planning, which will yield a more accurate picture of true need—and thereby enable local decision makers to allocate resources more effectively and efficiently systemwide. An Advanced Notice of Proposed Rulemaking that aligns the transit asset management process with the need for strengthening transit safety was published in October 2013. FTA is now reviewing the extensive comments received and plans to publish a Notice of Proposed Rulemaking guided by this input by early 2015. The purpose of a National Transit Asset Management System is to:

- Define a state of good repair.
- Establish a state-of-good-repair performance measure, and require funding recipients to set state-of-good-repair performance targets.
- Require recipients and subrecipients to develop a transit asset management plan.
- Add the reporting of capital asset inventories and conditions to the National Transit Database.

MAP–21 provided FTA additional tools to help the transit industry come to grips with its state-of-good-repair challenges. We fully recognize that to address the scope and complexity of this challenge, we need a range of policy tools at our disposal, including not only transit asset management, but also public–private partnerships such as the Denver Eagle project and innovative financing mechanisms, such as the Transportation Infrastructure Finance and Innovation Act (TIFIA) and the Railroad Rehabilitation & Improvement Financing Program (RRIF).

All of these actions, taken together, reflect the U.S. Department of Transportation's strategic commitment to address the infrastructure deficit in a holistic fashion—and to help the industry employ better metrics that enable them, in turn, to be better stewards of their assets. However, under MAP–21, our efforts still do not go far enough. The current State of Good Repair Formula Grant Program focuses on rail and bus rapid transit (BRT) systems that are at least 7 years old. The preservation needs of non-BRT bus services are not addressed in MAP–21. The need for additional investments and innovative policies that address the backlog for all bus and rail maintenance still exists, and much more work remains to be done—as the data in the C&P Report indicates, and as the President's FY2015 Budget and GROW AMERICA Act proposal make clear.

2013 C&P Report Substantiates Need for Further Investment

The 2013 C&P Report, which is based on 2010 data, makes a case rooted in facts that our Nation is falling behind on its obligation to maintain, preserve, and protect the transit assets serving thousands of communities nationwide today. The report finds that:

- Significant funding commitments are needed. As much as $24.5 billion in capital spending is needed per year from FY2011–FY2030 to improve the condition of transit rail and bus systems and support expansion to meet growing ridership needs. This is a nearly 50 percent increase over current capital spending levels from all government sources (Federal, State, and local).

  - Removing expansion investment from the equation, we need $18.5 billion in average annual investments (from all government sources) during the same period just to eliminate the current $86 billion maintenance backlog.
  - A minimum of $2.5 billion annually is needed just to maintain the status quo, that is, to prevent the current backlog from escalating further.
  - Our current rate of reinvestment (about $10.3 billion from all sources) is not sufficient to reduce the backlog in any meaningful way.

- Rail systems are heavily affected by the backlog. Rail systems collectively account for about 63 percent of the total state-of-good-repair backlog. Some transit systems are still operating rail cars that are over 30 years old, but the report also highlights that over 75 percent of the need for repairs affects other facets of transit rail infrastructure, such as rail stations, trestles, and power substations. Indeed, nonvehicle rail assets pose the biggest challenge to achieving a state of good repair.
- State and local governments bear the burden. State and local governments are shouldering more than half the cost of annual investments to preserve and grow the Nation's transit systems. Indeed, public funds made up nearly 75 percent of dollars expended on investments in capital projects and transit operations in 2010, with State and local sources leading the way.
- Preventive maintenance expenditures increasingly consume Federal grant funds. From 2000 to 2010, Federal funding for transit operating needs increased 360 percent. More than half of that—56 percent—was driven by capital grant funds used for preventive maintenance needs.

A key question that arises from the C&P Report data is why the transit maintenance backlog continues to grow, despite concerted efforts to chip away at it over the last several years. Various factors contribute to the continued increase, including the fact that, as transit agencies implement asset management best practices and improve their ability to conduct more detailed and accurate needs assessments, their reported data reveals a more fine-grained analysis of asset replacement needs and their costs. Additionally, the targeted investments made in recent years to address this problem simply do not match the depth of the infrastructure deficit overall, which has built up over decades of underinvestment.

The Administration Remains Committed To Addressing the Infrastructure Deficit

In his FY2015 budget request for the U.S. Department of Transportation and the FTA, President Obama builds on the commitment begun in MAP–21 with a request of $7.7 billion for the existing State of Good Repair Formula Grant Program and the Bus and Bus Facilities Grant Program. This represents an increase of $5.1 billion over the FY2014 funding levels for these two programs.

The Administration believes, in light of the history and data presented here and the progress made to date, that this increase is essential to help bring our national rail transit infrastructure into a state of good repair—while also enabling transit agencies to replace aging buses and bus facilities. (The increase on the rail side is $3.6 billion, or 164 percent, over FY2014 enacted levels; the increase on the bus side is $1.5 billion, or 353 percent, over FY2014 enacted levels.)

The FY2015 budget is a downpayment on a 4-year, $302 billion reauthorization proposal, known as the GROW AMERICA Act, which will strengthen surface transportation nationwide. The GROW AMERICA Act commits more than $72 billion over 4 years to address the urgent transit challenges facing urban, suburban and rural communities. The Act represents a nearly 70 percent increase in authorized transit funding over MAP–21.

In keeping with the momentum of MAP–21, the GROW AMERICA Act would provide $23 billion over 4 years (FY2015–FY2018) to continue efforts to address the transit industry's infrastructure deficit and maintenance backlog. By increasing the level of predictable funding for state-of-good-repair needs, transit agencies—along with State and local governments already shouldering more than half the cost of the annual investments to preserve and grow the Nation's transit systems—will be better positioned to provide safe, reliable transportation services to meet rising demand.

In addition, to address the critical need to replace aging bus fleets, which provide transportation to nearly half the transit riders in America, the GROW AMERICA Act would provide $7.8 billion in formula and discretionary funds over 4 years to ensure that communities have the resources needed to modernize bus fleets and facilities, lower repair bills, improve fuel efficiency, and better serve millions of riders. Nearly 40 percent of the Nation's buses and bus facilities are in marginal or poor condition—as the examples cited above illustrate—and significant investment is needed to bring them into a state of good repair. This proposal remedies an acknowledged shortfall in MAP–21 and helps put bus fleets on the path to modernization.

In closing, the investment in public transportation's future that we need to make is an investment in thousands of good jobs in communities nationwide that help to strengthen middle-class families; an investment in local economic growth and neighborhood revitalization; an investment in reducing roadway congestion that plagues so many metropolitan areas; an investment in lowering our dependence on foreign oil; and an investment in helping our Nation compete with the rest of the world as we find new and better ways to move people efficiently and safely.

We recognize that striking an appropriate balance between growing our transportation infrastructure to meet future demand and reinvesting in our current system is not easy to achieve. It will require targeted investments from all sources—Federal, State, local, and the private sector—to make meaningful changes.

Mr. Chairman, this concludes my testimony and I would be happy to answer any questions.

———

PREPARED STATEMENT OF JOSEPH M. CASEY

GENERAL MANAGER, SOUTHEASTERN PENNSYLVANIA TRANSPORTATION AUTHORITY, PHILADELPHIA, PENNSYLVANIA

MAY 22, 2014

Chairman Menendez, Ranking Member Moran, and Members of the Subcommittee, thank you for the opportunity to testify on the Federal role in bringing the Nation's public transportation infrastructure to a state of good repair. I am Joseph Casey, General Manager of the Southeastern Pennsylvania Transportation Authority (SEPTA).

About SEPTA

SEPTA was formed by an act of the Pennsylvania General Assembly to provide public transportation services to the five counties of southeastern Pennsylvania (Bucks, Chester, Delaware, Montgomery, and Philadelphia). Between 1964 and 1983, SEPTA assumed ownership and operation of various transportation companies, including the Philadelphia Transit Company (PTC), the Philadelphia and Western Railroad (the P&W or Red Arrow), and a commuter railroad system from Conrail that was originally constructed by the Pennsylvania and Reading Railroads. Today, SEPTA is the sixth largest public transportation operator in the country, and the largest in Pennsylvania.

SEPTA's service territory covers 2,220 square miles and four million residents living in the five-county region, with service extending to Trenton and West Trenton, New Jersey and Newark, Delaware. SEPTA is a multimodal transit system which provides a vast network of fixed-route services including 119 bus routes, two subway/subway elevated lines, 13 Regional Rail lines, eight trolley lines, three trackless trolley routes, an interurban high-speed rail line, and paratransit service. SEPTA provides more than one million daily passenger trips, and during the fiscal year that ended June 30, 2013, SEPTA recorded 337.3 million (unlinked) passenger trips. Regional Rail ridership has increased 50 percent, over the last 15 years, with annual ridership up from 24 million to an all-time record 36 million trips last year. Ridership continues to grow across all modes, with average annual increases of 1.9 percent over the last 7 years, and total annual trips up by more than 40 million since 2006.

Our Nation's economic competitiveness and long-term prosperity rely upon the ability of its extensive and interconnected transportation network to safely and efficiently move people and commerce throughout the country, and connect U.S. markets to the world. Maintaining the infrastructure that supports the Nation's highway, transit, freight and intercity passenger rail systems is an established national priority, and Congress must preserve the Federal Government's 50-plus year commitment to public transportation, and preserve and strengthen the Mass Transit Account of the Highway Trust Fund.

Last year, Americans took 10.7 billion trips on public transportation. Yet, at a time when transit ridership reached its highest levels in 57 years, the industry continues to fall behind in the investment required to bring our transit systems to a state of good repair.

According to the 2013 Conditions and Performance Report released by the U.S. Department of Transportation in February, the state-of-good-repair backlog for transit systems nationwide has risen to $86 billion—an increase of $9 billion, or nearly 12 percent, since the FTA's 2010 National State of Good Repair Assessment. This number is projected to grow by $2.5 billion per year, and the Report states that total spending on state of good repair from all sources must increase by $8.2 billion per year to address this backlog.

The funding and operational pressures related to state of good repair are particularly acute for large urban transit systems with aging rail infrastructure. Infrastructure related to rail transportation—track, power equipment, bridges and tunnels, stations and vehicles—accounts for roughly three quarters of the national transit state-of-good-repair backlog. It is important to note that older systems—such as ours in Philadelphia—were built largely without the benefit of Federal support.

In MAP–21, Congress responded to the rail state-of-good-repair crisis by creating the new state-of-good-repair grant program and increasing funding for the Nation's rail transit systems to invest in their critical state-of-good-repair needs.

On behalf of transit riders in our region, I want to thank this Committee for its role in making that program a reality. Creating that program was a major goal for SEPTA and our colleagues in other regions. In pursuit of that goal, leaders of the Nation's largest transit systems formed in 2007 an informal group we call the Metropolitan Rail Discussion Group (MRDG). Since 2010, I have served as Chair of MRDG. Our basic principles include the following:

- Passage of a 6-year transportation authorization with predictable, growing sources of funding.
- Increased Federal investment to modernize our Nation's public rail transportation systems given their significant impact on issues of national importance such as jobs, economic development, congestion relief, and air quality.
- Funding within the Federal transit program should be prioritized according to need and with consideration of the impact of that funding on the issues of national importance.

It is important to emphasize that first principle—a predictable and growing source of funding. As I noted earlier, the state-of-good-repair backlog is growing quickly at our Nation's transit systems. Our investment, therefore, must also increase so we do not fall farther behind.

Our experience at SEPTA demonstrates the need for investment and the cost of not investing. Our current backlog of unmet infrastructure needs is now more than $5 billion dollars—nearly three-quarters of which is concentrated in SEPTA's aging rail infrastructure. SEPTA's Regional Rail and rail transit network is extensive, and much of the infrastructure that supports it has exceeded its useful life and requires replacement. For example:

- Much of SEPTA's Regional Rail system was originally built in the mid-to-late-19th century. The average age of SEPTA's railroad bridges is more than 80 years old, with 103 bridges that are more than 100 years old.
- Fifteen of SEPTA's 20 traction power substations responsible for powering large segments of the Regional Rail system have been in continuous operation for more than 80 years, and are still relying on technology originally developed in the 1920s.
- The Authority's 231 Silverliner IV railcars (representing approximately two-thirds of SEPTA's Regional Rail fleet) are nearly 40 years old. More than 150 city and suburban trolley cars have already exceeded their 30-year useful life, and will need to be replaced within 10 years.

Over the next decade, SEPTA will need to invest $6.5 billion—approximately $650 million per year—just to bring the system to a state of good repair, including:

- $572 million to repair power substations and other power infrastructure
- $716 million on systemwide track and tie renewal
- $1.2 billion on systemwide Regional Rail and rail transit station rehabilitation and ADA improvements
- $976 million for critical bridge replacement, rehabilitation, and maintenance

• $2 billion on rail vehicle replacement

These cost realities are further exacerbated by funding pressures created by several unfunded Federal mandates, including Positive Train Control (PTC), and changes included in the Passenger Rail Investment and Improvement Act (PRIIA) that increase fees paid to Amtrak.

• SEPTA made a commitment to achieving full compliance with the PTC mandate and is on schedule to make the December 31, 2015, implementation deadline. However, in doing so, SEPTA will ultimately divert more than $305 million away from critical state-of-good-repair projects, including bridge and power substation rehabilitation.
• Starting in Federal Fiscal Year 2015, SEPTA's annual capital and operating contribution requirements for rights to operate over Amtrak territory were increased as a result of language in PRIIA.

The cumulative effect of growing needs and level funding creates challenges to maintaining safe and efficient transit operations. By focusing on safety and adopting a ''fix-it-first'' approach, the Authority has been successful in sustaining service levels and ontime performance by directing capital resources to its most critically deficient infrastructure. This investment approach has guided our use of Federal funds in recent years from MAP–21 and the American Recovery and Reinvestment Act (ARRA). Here are some examples of how we have invested the funds Congress has made available to us:

American Recovery and Reinvestment Act—SEPTA has a strong track record of implementing capital projects quickly, especially after being awarded Federal funding from nontraditional sources. This is best exemplified by SEPTA's execution of its American Reinvestment and Recovery Act (ARRA) projects. SEPTA received $191 million in ARRA funds and advanced 32 projects. All major construction contracts were awarded within 1 year; and all projects were completed in less than 3 years.

Wayne Junction Regional Rail Substation—Built in 1931 for the old Reading Railroad lines, Wayne Junction Substation is a central facility that distributes electricity to 11 outlying substations and feeds catenary wires for half of SEPTA's Regional Rail lines. A failure at the Wayne Junction Substation would cause major disruption throughout the entire regional rail network. In partnership with the City of Philadelphia and the Pennsylvania Department of Transportation (PennDOT), SEPTA was awarded $12.8 million in funding through the Federal 2012 Transportation Investment Generating Economic Recovery (TIGER) program for the renovation of the 80-year-old Substation. State and local sources provided matching funding in the amount of $12.9. Construction is underway on this critical project.

Hybrid Bus Replacement—SEPTA's current fleet of more than 1,400 buses includes 472 diesel-electric hybrid buses—approximately one-third of the total fleet. SEPTA was successful in securing Federal competitive grants to assist in funding its hybrid bus replacement program. SEPTA expects to take delivery of an additional 205 hybrid buses, continuing to make SEPTA one of the largest public transit operators of this cleaner more efficient engine technology.

Silverliner V Railcar Procurement—SEPTA was able to leverage former FTA Section 5309 formula funding to secure the issuance of GARVEE Bonds that financed the purchase of 120 new Regional Rail cars to replace cars which were more than 40 years old and exceeded their useful life. The new railcars fully comply with American with Disabilities (ADA) requirements and meet Federal Railroad Administration (FRA) passenger car strength and safety requirements. Final assembly of the new cars took place at the Hyundai-Rotem facility in South Philadelphia where up to 300 jobs, including those of mechanics and electricians, were created to assemble the cars. Without a long-term Federal formula program, SEPTA would not have been able to utilize this funding mechanism to make this important safety and efficiency upgrade to its rail fleet.

Climate Change Adaptation Assessment Pilot Program—In 2011, SEPTA was selected for funding as one of seven pilot projects undertaken through the Federal Transit Administration's Climate Change Adaptation Assessment Pilot Program. The recommendations of the FTA Pilot Program report, which are now codified within SEPTA's ''Standard Readiness Plan for Hurricanes'', are the foundation of SEPTA's Hurricane Sandy Resiliency Grant application. The grant application included 15 selected projects which will reinforce power systems for critical facilities, stabilize embankments prone to erosion, restore track integrity, improve hydrologic conditions, and prevent infrastructure degradation due to water infiltration. The application reflects SEPTA's overarching goal to improve resilience against costly damage and passenger delays, and to ensure ongoing continuity of operations, in the event of known and emergent vulnerabilities associated with extreme weather.

Of course, the Federal Government provides only a portion of the funds required to maintain and improve our transit system. The Commonwealth of Pennsylvania is a critical partner for us as well.

In Pennsylvania, Governor Tom Corbett and bipartisan leaders in the Pennsylvania General Assembly authored a comprehensive transportation funding plan that provides dedicated and growing investment in the State's transportation infrastructure. Transit infrastructure rehabilitation was one of the cornerstones of the bill, and funding was made available for SEPTA to begin to address its most urgent infrastructure needs.

Our story in Pennsylvania is not unique. My colleagues in other regions are working to address the state-of-good-repair backlog through the resources of their own State and local governments as well. Indeed, the DOT report referenced previously notes that in 2013, State and local governments shouldered more than half the burden for investment in state of good repair for public transportation. Our leaders are doing this because they recognize the high cost of inaction.

We had to illustrate clearly the cost of inaction in order to build support for the Pennsylvania funding plan. As the bill was being discussed, the Authority was developing a plan that would have realigned the SEPTA system to service levels that could be safely supported under the constraints of persistent, long-term capital funding shortfalls. This realignment plan was necessary because of 4 years of severely reduced capital budgets and long-range funding uncertainty. If the plan had been implemented, more than 88,000 daily rail passenger trips would have been eliminated over the next decade. The congestion impacts would have been staggering.

The legislature recognized this was not a "Chicken Little" plan. It was a sober look at the cost of not investing in our transportation networks. That is a key point I want to make to this Subcommittee today: we spend too much time focusing on the cost of Government programs for infrastructure and not enough time focusing on the crippling cost of NOT investing in infrastructure.

In southeastern Pennsylvania, SEPTA is the engine of the regional and State economy, providing more than one million daily passenger trips. SEPTA has achieved record ridership during a national economic downturn, in spite of stagnant capital funding that has delayed systemwide improvements, and without expanding service. This ridership growth reveals two things: residents of southeastern Pennsylvania are increasingly choosing public transportation as their principal mobility option, and SEPTA's effective use of public investment is paying great dividends in customer satisfaction and rider retention.

To understand the entire cost of not investing, though, we need to look beyond ridership impact to the broader economic benefits of public transportation in our major metro areas. These areas rely on public transportation to fuel economic growth and competitiveness by connecting employees to their jobs, allowing freight and vehicle commuters to move on less congested highways, and providing important mobility options for all members of the community.

While the benefits of investing in our system are mostly felt by the people and businesses in our service area, the economic impact of SEPTA transcends our regional boundaries.

SEPTA's capital and operating expenditures contribute $3.21 billion in economic output, supporting nearly 26,000 jobs. Hundreds of companies—large and small—across Pennsylvania and the country also benefit from doing business with SEPTA. Each year, SEPTA procurement returns hundreds of millions of dollars to the national economy, supporting business and creating jobs. Between 2009 and 2012, SEPTA purchased more than $1 billion in goods and services from Pennsylvania companies, and an additional $850 million from businesses throughout the country.

The Nation's economy is damaged when our major metro areas cease to function efficiently as gateways for the movement of goods and people between U.S. and international destinations. A short-term "patch" on the Highway Trust Fund highway and transit accounts will not address the crucial shortfall in investment. If Congress takes that approach—either for 6 months, a year, or 2 years—it will be sending a signal to State and local officials that they do not have a partner in Washington.

Now more than ever, States need to know they have a strong and committed Federal partner in the preservation of the Nation's transportation infrastructure.

With all these points in mind, I urge this Subcommittee and the full Committee to develop a plan for a multiyear public transportation investment program with funding levels that show increases from year-to-year to reflect the growing needs across the country. A robust and growing state-of-good-repair program should be a centerpiece of the national transit program.

Thank you for the opportunity to testify today and I look forward to answering your questions.

———

PREPARED STATEMENT OF BEVERLY A. SCOTT
GENERAL MANAGER AND CHIEF EXECUTIVE OFFICER, MASSACHUSETTS BAY TRANSPORTATION AUTHORITY

MAY 22, 2014

Chairman Menendez, Ranking Member Moran, and Members of the Committee, thank you for inviting me to testify before you today on this important issue. The Massachusetts Bay Transportation Authority is the fifth largest transit provider in the United States, with more than 1.3 million passenger trips per day and in excess of 395 million trips per year. The MBTA system is the original and oldest transit network in the U.S., with the subway opening in 1897 and expanding throughout the 20th century. The commuter rail system was originally laid out in the 1830s as some of the first railroads in the U.S. Some of the MBTA bus facilities date to the early 20th century, having been initially designed to serve horse-drawn omnibuses. With this great history in transit comes some of the oldest and in many cases outdated infrastructure. Operating this important network in a State of Good Repair (SGR) is a significant challenge for the MBTA and for which we are heavily engaged with our Federal partners at the FTA to work with us to keep this system operating in a safe, reliable, accessible, and sustainable manner.

Under the leadership of Governor Patrick, Massachusetts has taken great steps to address the growing SGR backlog that existed at the MBTA. The backlog encompasses all those assets that are past their useful lives and in need of investment for replacement/renewal (e.g., vehicles, bridges, tracks, stations, facilities, power, signal, and communication systems, etc.). When Governor Patrick came into office in 2007, the MBTA's SGR backlog was upwards of $5 billion, with only a small portion of that funded annually through our capital program. The Patrick administration recognized that this issue is one that cannot be further deferred and has taken action to implement important transportation reforms. These reforms include employee health care, retirement benefits, and other administrative programs that are designed to maximize efficiencies, eliminate redundancy, incorporate innovative technology, and focus on sustainability to bring stability to rising transit costs and limited revenues.

After launching these comprehensive transportation reforms, Governor Patrick proposed the Way Forward program to provide the necessary funding for the transportation system. Governor Patrick worked with the Massachusetts Legislature to implement strategies that generate new State revenues dedicated to funding transportation. These new revenues include the first increase in over 20 years of the State gasoline tax. This increase is aligned with inflation to ensure that the level of funding will keep pace over time. The plan was approved by the Legislature in 2013 and will generate over $800 million in new revenue for transportation, which, when leveraged, will support $2.6 billion to address the MBTA's SGR backlog over the next decade. The Way Forward Program provides reliable and predictable revenue to address the most pressing needs of the MBTA, which include new vehicles, upgraded track, electric traction power, signal and communications improvements as well as investments in bridges and facilities.

While focusing on the present, the Governor has continued to look toward the future by investing in new projects. One notable project is the Green Line Extension, which we anticipate will receive a 50 percent funding grant from the FTA's New Starts Program. This transformative project will bring transportation, land use, environmental and economic development benefits to areas currently under served by transit.

The MBTA has allocated funding with a focus on safety, security, and service reliability. We have also focused our investments to create secondary benefits, such as promoting private commercial and residential development at transit stations. We have also focused on developing infrastructure that will consume less energy, investments to make the system more accessible to people with disabilities and to an aging population, and making the system more resilient to extreme storms and the oncoming effects of climate change.

Additionally, the MBTA has changed the way we make decisions on future investments, and implemented systems to track and measure those investments. We have developed tools to focus our long term capital investment decisions, including a strong asset management program and SGR database. Consistent with MAP–21, we have integrated an overall focus on investment outcomes, using performance metrics and other tools to measure the value of investments.

It is important not to lose site of the nexus between our SGR and a skilled future workforce. We need to ensure that tomorrow's workers have the skills and training necessary to build, install and maintain this equipment, such as signals and communications, power systems, engineering, information technology and the other fields that we will rely on even more in the future to build and maintain this infrastructure.

The MBTA recognizes the need for fiscal responsibility when it comes to funding our SGR backlog. We anticipate spending nearly $6 billion over the next 5 years, with more than 60 percent of those funds being local funds. Despite the significant local investment, there is a critical need—particularly for older rail agencies—for a strong and robust Federal investment in SGR. As we face record-high transit ridership on increasingly aging systems, reaffirming the Federal commitment to the millions of Americans who ride public transportation is more essential than ever. Transit agencies across the country see an increased need for vigorous Federal funding in the next surface transportation authorization bill given that Federal investment in transportation is an investment in American jobs, American communities, American strategies to address climate change and American economic competitiveness.

Delivering safe, reliable, and accessible public transit has always been a partnership between public sector agencies at all levels of government working with communities and stakeholders. While the MBTA and many other transit agencies have made significant investments using local funds, a reliable and predictable level of Federal funding is needed if we are going to seriously address the significant SGR backlog faced by transit agencies such as the MBTA. We are hopeful that this Congress, through its upcoming Transportation Reauthorization Bill, can begin to address this critical need by supporting the funding levels that were proposed in the Administration's reauthorization proposal.

Thank you for this opportunity to testify and I am happy to take any questions you may have.

PREPARED STATEMENT OF GARY THOMAS

PRESIDENT AND EXECUTIVE DIRECTOR, DALLAS AREA RAPID TRANSIT

MAY 22, 2014

Thank you Mr. Chairman. My name is Gary Thomas and I am the President/Executive Director of Dallas Area Rapid Transit (DART). DART was created on August 13, 1983, when North Texans in and around the city of Dallas voted to commit 1 percent local sales taxes to fund public transportation. Today DART is a multimodal transit agency operating North America's longest light rail system in the fourth largest metropolitan area in the United States. DART provided approximately 2.3 million people inside its 13 city, 700-square mile service area with around 107 million total transit trips in FY2013 through our bus, light rail, commuter rail, HOV, Paratransit, and Van Pool programs.

State of Good Repair Is a DART Priority

As DART continues maturing as a transit operator, a significant portion of the agency's expenses will shift to the maintenance and replacement of infrastructure and vehicles. In fact, approximately 73 percent of DART's capital spending over the next 20 years is dedicated to State-of-Good-Repair (SGR) projects. This is due to an agency policy—in place since our creation—that mandates we balance the expenses of operations, asset management, and capital expansion through a 20-Year Financial Plan.

The financial planning parameters provide the foundation for the ongoing balance and recalibration of capital systems expansion, operating costs, and asset condition and replacement. This has allowed DART to meet the challenge of both maintaining the operational readiness of our current assets while meeting our commitments to the region for further expansion of the transportation network. Between 2001 and 2010, DART doubled its light rail system twice, despite a regional economy that was experiencing double-digit unemployment and flat or lesser sales tax revenue. In other words, the expansion was carried out, and infrastructure maintained, with no growth in the source that represents approximately 75 percent of the agency's annual revenue.

Even amidst the worst national economic crisis since the Great Depression, DART has been fortunate to continue to move forward with major capital projects by following the guidance of its financial plan developed by these sound planning parameters. The 28-mile Green Line, which received a $700 million Full Funding Grant

Agreement under the Federal Transit Administration's New Starts program in 2006, was completed and in revenue service by late 2010. Additionally, both the Orange Line and Blue Line extensions were completed and in revenue service in 2012. Improving local economic conditions and the success of our multiyear financial and budgetary initiatives have made possible the acceleration by three years of the South Oak Cliff Blue Line extension to the University of North Texas-Dallas campus. Finally, DART is currently replacing our entire bus fleet with new compressed natural gas fueled vehicles. This began in the fall of 2012 and will be complete in 2016.

The DART Approach to State of Good Repair

DART has well over 15 years of asset condition assessment experience. The commitment to a regular interval of assessment by a trained team of internal assessors has provided DART with sound comparative data to determine adequacy of our long range financial, maintenance, and asset replacement plans.

One of the key elements of DART's SGR program is the Asset Condition Study. The goals of this regularly scheduled asset assessment are: to obtain high level assessment of the inventory of assets; provide comparative results to previous assessments; ensure rate of physical degradation is consistent with plan; validate maintenance and financial plans are aligned with assessment results; and support adjustment of maintenance and financial plans where necessary. Included in any successful SGR program is the assessment of technology and reconciling the need for its replacement due to obsolescence.

In addition, DART's capital program request process employs a multidimensional assessment of each project request based on industry standard risk analysis concepts modified to consider factors of financial and operational risk, as well as, customer risk/benefits. This multidimensional analysis is used to prioritize each project request and is particularly useful in times of volatile funding levels like those experienced over the past decade. DART is currently evaluating software which allows for modeling of the various future program requirements against differing future revenue streams to aid leadership team decisions going forward.

Lessons learned from this experience include, but are not limited to: using consistent process and scoring systems; documentation of the method of data capture, storage and analysis of the data; and, analysis of assets from an overall subgroup perspective.

MAP–21 SGR Policy Implementation

Even before the enactment of MAP–21, which made SGR national transit policy, DART has worked side-by-side with the FTA and our transit industry partners to improve the understanding and practice of transit asset management. In its 2010 National State of Good Repair Assessment, the FTA found that more than 40 percent of bus assets and 25 percent of rail transit assets were in marginal or poor condition. Additionally, there is an estimated backlog of $50 to $80 billion in deferred maintenance and replacement needs, of which the vast majority is rail related. This backlog continues to grow at a rate of approximately $3.5B annually.

The enactment of MAP–21 places the requirement on transit agencies to prepare a Transit Asset Management Plan. Transit agency customers, policy makers, and public agencies are holding agency management accountable for performance and increasingly expect more business-like management practices. The magnitude of capital needs, performance expectations, and increased accountability requires transit agency managers to enhance their approach to asset management.

To advance the practice of transit asset management, the FTA created the "Asset Management Guide". This guide provides a transit specific asset management framework for managing assets individually and as a portfolio of assets that comprise an integrated system. The guide provides flexible, yet targeted guidance to advance the practice and implementation of transit asset management.

MAP–21 made SGR national policy and the FTA has sought comments from industry partners through the administrative rulemaking process. DART believes the Federal Government should allow the FTA to implement the policy as mandated by MAP–21, and allow the industry time to adjust to the new policies as implemented, prior to making any major policy revisions in a new surface transportation bill.

The Need for a Core Capacity Program

State of Good Repair. Capital investments are not always about system additions or expansions. DART has significantly increased light rail infrastructure over the past 10 years, we have also increased our SGR obligations to maintain and replace those assets. DART's current light rail system configuration merges all rail lines (Red, Blue, Orange, and Green) within Dallas' Central Business District. As a consequence of heavy use and growth of the light rail system since DART first began light rail operations in 1996, the track condition along this 1.25-mile long rail corridor has deteriorated more quickly than DART had previously anticipated.

Coupled with the rapid growth of the light rail system and passenger loads reaching approximately 100,000 passengers per day, we have determined that to maintain a State of Good Repair, the rail in our downtown core will need to be replaced within the next 2 years, well ahead of what was previously thought to be its useful life. This project, which directly impacts the ongoing reliability of the existing network, will require an investment approaching $45 to $50 million, and funding has been provided within the FY2014 Budget and 20-Year Financial Plan.

Core Capacity. While DART will continue to aggressively invest annually to ensure a SGR, we recognize the need for a program designed to provide congestion relief and help address capacity needs of a rail corridor. Let me be very clear, DART is a strong advocate for a federally funded core capacity program and very interested in preserving it as a part of the Capital Investment Program as authorized by MAP–21. DART has been developing a core capacity strategy that could be advanced through the FTA Capital Investment Program. This strategy develops a program of interrelated projects which will be critical to respond to continued high regional growth trends, demands for system accessibility, expansion of new rail corridors outside our Service Area, and the development of a privately funded high speed rail system between Dallas and Houston, which is anticipated to open in 2021.

The DART Board of Directors is currently in the process of initiating a long-range (2040) system plan update to outline future capital programs in addition to the core capacity program of interrelated projects. This update will strive to meet future regional growth expectations. In order for our system to fully integrate and accommodate the expected passenger demand, DART will need to advance both a second light rail alignment in the Dallas central business district and extend many of its current station platforms along the Red and Blue lines to accommodate longer trains. These projects will increase the core capacity of our system and enable it to be more sustainable and flexible in the long-term. Both of these projects are typical of core capacity needs not only in Dallas but across the country. We need a strong Federal core capacity program to support our efforts.

As our ridership continues to grow, we will be operating near or in excess of our physical capacity, and above a level that provides acceptable passenger comfort and convenience. Without significant capital investment to expand the core capacity of the system, it is likely that DART will be unable to address growing demands in a fashion suitable to our customers and stakeholders.

Conclusion

With the enactment of MAP–21 in 2012, the Federal Government identified the need for sound financial planning and asset management practices throughout the transit industry. The FTA estimated in its 2010 National State of Good Repair Assessment that the Nation's transit systems have a state-of-good-repair backlog of almost $78 billion in deferred maintenance and replacement needs. DART has worked diligently with the FTA, other key transportation authorities, and the American Public Transportation Association to craft national guidelines for this Federal policy based substantially on the practices DART has employed since its inception in 1983. MAP–21 also created a specific ''State of Good Repair'' grant program to help fund this mandate. DART recommends the continuation and growth of the program in the next surface transportation authorization.

Finally, DART supports any and all efforts made by the Federal Government to provide more stable funding to support national transportation programs. DART applauds the bipartisan leadership of the Senate Environment and Works Committee for its 6-year highway bill and we look forward to working with the Banking Committee as it develops its transit title in the next bill. Toward that end, we appreciate the leadership of Transportation Secretary Foxx in the proposed ''GROW America'' legislation and hope the Committee will give it consideration, as well as the recommendations of the American Public Transportation Association, as you draft the transit title. Stable, predictable, and dedicated transit funding is critical to DART services. The most relevant challenge to DART's financial approach has been the volatility in the predictability of future revenues. DART relies heavily on transit formula funds, which are used to purchase rail cars and buses, improve maintenance and passenger facilities, as well as rebuild vehicles, track, and signalization systems. These funds also put decision making in the hands of local officials, allowing for focused investment where it is needed most in order to maintain passenger safety and improve efficiency.

In conclusion, Mr. Chairman, on behalf of the 3,700 employees at DART, I would like to thank you for the opportunity you have given me here today. I stand ready to answer any questions you or any of the other Members of the Subcommittee may have.

36

STATEMENT SUBMITTED BY LEANNE P. REDDEN, ACTING EXECUTIVE DIRECTOR, CHICAGO REGIONAL TRANSPORTATION AUTHORITY

Regional Transportation Authority

Statement for the Record

Chicago Regional Transportation Authority

Senate Banking Committee

Bringing Our Transit Infrastructure to a State of Good Repair

May 22, 2014

175 W. Jackson Blvd,
Suite 1650
Chicago, IL 60604
312-913-3200
rtachicago.org

The Northeastern Illinois Regional Transportation Authority's (RTA) primary responsibilities are overseeing regional transit planning issues and the financial and budget oversight of the Chicago Transit Authority (CTA), Metra commuter rail and Pace suburban bus.

Another important function of the RTA is the development of the annual five-year capital plan, which is a blueprint for the capital activities to be funded by the RTA and executed by the CTA, Metra and Pace.

As the agency responsible for overseeing the financing and planning for public transportation in the Northeastern Illinois region, the RTA has a complete picture of the consequences of underinvestment. The investment that would be required to bring the region's capital assets to a State of Good Repair (SGR) today would be roughly $20 billion. On top of the $20 billion one-time SGR investment, the normal capital reinvestment that includes no expansion and no new projects would be $1.34 billion per year (for a total of $13.4 billion over 10 years), which means over the next 10 years the regional SGR need is going to amount to $33.4 billion.

The lack of federal funding to address the SGR backlog is significantly problematic for transit systems across America. According to a 2013 Conditions and Performance Report, the U.S. SGR backlog is $86 billion and projected to grow by $2 billion per year if the current underinvestment in U.S. transit systems continues.

Addressing the SGR backlog through federal investment is not just good policy, it is critical to the United States economy. A recent study released by the American Public Transportation Association "demonstrates that investment in public transportation will lead to 50,700 jobs per $1 billion invested, with 28,900 jobs per $1 billion attributed to the productivity gains enjoyed by households and businesses." While underinvestment in transit assets inevitably leads some to assume safety may be compromised, the true concern for the transit systems is reliability.

Without reliability, transit operators do not have a system its customers can depend on for getting to work, running everyday errands or attending social events. This unreliability could eventually lead to a strain on other parts of a given region's transportation system. There is no doubt the impact on the economy from underinvestment in addressing SGR is real.

The RTA was encouraged by the creation of the State of Good Repair formula program in the Moving Ahead for Progress in the 21st Century (MAP-21) Act, the most recent surface transportation authorization bill. However, if the federal government is serious about addressing the SGR backlog, funding levels addressing these needs will need to be robustly increased.

When the Administration released their surface transportation proposal, the GROW AMERICA Act, in late April, the RTA was heartened by the increased funding for public transportation, especially the increase for the State of Good Repair Grants. The RTA believes the almost 167% increase from FY 2014 SGR enacted levels under the GROW AMERICA Act is the type of federal effort that is needed to address the serious national backlog.

The RTA understands the constrained funding realities of the federal surface transportation program due to its current revenue structure. This understanding has lead the agency to work with national coalition groups like Getting America to Work that support increased federal investment in public transportation—RTA is aware that members of Congress have less reason to support increased federal funding in public transportation if they are not hearing from their constituents about the negative economic impact of underinvestment.

Overseeing the third largest public transportation system in the United States has provided the RTA with an appreciation of the significant backlog of SGR needs. The RTA is committed to working with Congress and the Administration in any way to strengthen the program's funding levels which will help grow our economy through getting people where they need to go in an efficient and reliable manner.

Please feel free to use the RTA as a resource as your Committee continues to proceed with the reauthorization of MAP-21.

Sincerely,

Leanne P. Redden
Acting Executive Director